Keto Slow Cooker Cookbook For Everyone

The Complete Guide to Cook Healthy and Easy Ketogenic Slow Cooker Recipes For Yourself & Family

D1719890

Jasmine Reyes

Disclaimer Notice:

Please note the information contained within this document is for educational and entertainment purposes only. All effort has been executed to present accurate, up to date, and reliable, complete information. No warranties of any kind are declared or implied. Readers acknowledge that the author is not engaging in the rendering of legal, financial, medical or professional advice. The content within this book has been derived from various sources. Please consult a licensed professional before attempting any techniques outlined in this book.

By reading this document, the reader agrees that under no circumstances is the author responsible for any losses, direct or indirect, which are incurred as a result of the use of information contained within this document, including, but not limited to, errors, omissions, or inaccuracies.

Table of Content

INTRODUCTION 9

BREAKFAST RECIPES 11
    ALMOND LEMON BLUEBERRY MUFFINS 12
    CREAMY OREGANO CHORIZO MUSHROOM 14
    MACADAMIA NUT SQUARE 16
    MOZZARELLA BAGELS 18
    CREAM CHEESE BLUEBERRY MUFFINS 20

LUNCH RECIPES 22
    MEATBALLS WITH COCONUT GRAVY 23
    FRESH DAL 25
    BUTTERNUT SQUASH SOUP 27
    EGGPLANT BACON WRAPS 29

DINNER RECIPES 31
    CHIPOTLE BARBACOA 32
    CORNED BEEF CABBAGE ROLLS 34

MAIN 37
    GERMAN STYLE SOUP 37
    HERB MIXED RADISH 38
    TUSCAN CHICKEN 40
    CORNED BEEF 42

SOUPS, STEWS, AND CHILIS 44
    VEGETABLE BEEF SOUP 45
    LAMB TACO SOUP 47
    BUFFALO SAUCE 49
    HOISIN SAUCE 50
    MEXICAN POT ROAST 51
    EGG, SPINACH, AND MUSHROOM SLOW COOKER CASSEROLE 53
    WHITE BEAN SOUP WITH SHRIMP 55

VEGETABLES 57
    PECAN KALE MIX 58
    MUSHROOM SOUP 59
    ARTICHOKE AND ASPARAGUS MIX 61

LIME GREEN BEANS.. 62
CHEESE ASPARAGUS 63

MEAT 64

BEEF ROAST 65
LUNCH BEEF 67
GARLIC HERB PORK... 69
GARLIC THYME LAMBCHOPS.. 70

SIDE DISH RECIPES..71

TARRAGON SWEET POTATOES 71
CLASSIC VEGGIES MIX 73
GREEN BEANS AND MUSHROOMS.. 74
BEANS AND RED PEPPERS... 75

APPETIZERS & SNACKS..76

ASPARAGUS BACON BOUQUET... 77
CREAMY ASIAGO SPINACH DIP 78
MADRAS CURRY CHICKEN BITES... 80
SPICED JICAMA WEDGES WITH CILANTRO CHUTNEY 82
TERIYAKI CHICKENWINGS.. 84
PORTABELLA PIZZA BITES... 85

DESSERTS 87

LEMON CURD - KETO, LOW CARB & SUGAR-FREE....................... 88
EASY LEMON COCONUT CUSTARD PIE WITH COCONUT MILK 90
KETO CHOCOLATE AND HAZELNUT SPREAD 92
KETO BUTTERCREAM 94
KETO CARAMEL SAUCE 95
SIMPLE LOW-CARB CHOCOLATE TART (SUGAR-FREE)................. 97
EASY LEMON COCONUT CUSTARD PIE WITH COCONUT MILK 99

Introduction

Thank you for purchasing **Keto Slow Cooker Cookbook For Everyone: The Complete Guide to Cook Healthy and Easy Ketogenic Slow Cooker Recipes For Yourself & Family**

Having a slow stove is an effortless, fast and more flexible method of cooking in any home. It doesn't require any cooking skills; it saves your time because the slow cooker does all the work time for you, it's really safe and it can also be used in any place like a hotel room or even a student dorm because it has a kettle like shape, making it more portable than a stove. So, in the following guides, we will discuss some of the basic ways that are useful to ensure that you get the best out of your slow stove.

What it is.

The slow cooker appeared in 1970 and was marketed as a bean pot. But as it was modified, people started using it to reheat food and keep it warm for extended periods. And look how far we've come: people are cooking delicious, healthy meals with it. It's a perfect little kitchen appliance that consists of a glass lid, porcelain or ceramic pot (it's inside the heating unit) and, of course, a heating element. The modern Slow Cooker can be oval or round in shape and various sizes from small to large. All Slow Cookers have two settings: LOW (corresponds to a temperature of 200°F mostly) and HIGH (up to 300°F). The WARM selection found among most slow cooker options these days allows you to keep prepared dishes warm for a long time. Some slow cooker models have a timer that will allow you to control the cooking time if you are busy.

Breakfast Recipes

Almond Lemon Blueberry Muffins

Preparation Time: 17 minutes

Cooking time: 2-3 hours on High

Servings: 3

Ingredients:

- 1 cup almond flour

- 1 large egg

- 3 drops Stevia

- ¼ cup fresh blueberries

- ¼ teaspoon lemon zest, grated

- ¼ teaspoon pure lemon extract

- ½ cup heavy whipping cream

- 2 tablespoons butter, melted

- ½ teaspoon baking powder

Directions:

1. Add egg into a bowl. Whisk well

2. Add the rest of the ingredients into the bowl of egg. Whisk well.

3. Pour batter into lined or greased muffin molds. Pour up to ¾ of the cup.

4.   Pour 6 ounces of water into the slow cooker. Place an aluminum foil at the bottom of the cooker. Place the muffin molds inside the cooker.

5.   Close the lid. Set cooker on 'High' option and timer for 2-3 hours.

6.   Let it cool in the cooker for a while.

7.   Remove from the cooker. Loosen the edges of the muffins. Invert on to a plate and serve.

Nutrition: calories 223, fat 21, carbs 5, protein 6

Creamy Oregano Chorizo Mushroom

Preparation Time: 10 minutes

Cooking time: 4 hours 30 minutes

Servings: 8

Ingredients:

- 4 bell peppers

- 3 tbsp oregano

- 2 large onions

- 1 lb fresh mushrooms of any kind

- 1 lb cream cheese

- 1 cup milk

- 2 eggs

- 1 lb chorizo style Mexican sausage

Directions:

1.   Slice the bell peppers into thick slices.

2.   Chop onion into large pieces.

3.   Halve or quarter-chop mushrooms depending on preference.

4.   Turn on the slow cooker to high and begin to brown the chorizo, allowing the grease to bubble.

5.	Cook onions, peppers, and mushrooms for a few moments in chorizo grease.

6.	Combine the creamed cheese, oregano, milk, and eggs until blended smoothly. Pour milk and egg mixture on top of the meat in the slow cooker and set to low heat. Cover and let cook for four hours. Serve hot and enjoy!

Nutrition: calories 516, fat 10, carbs 11, protein 22

Macadamia Nut Square

Preparation Time: 10 minutes 1 hour chilling

Cooking Time: 0 minutes

Servings: 4

Ingredients:

- ¼ cup macadamia nuts

- ¼ cup nut butter

- 1 teaspoon erythritol

- 2 tablespoons butter, melted

- 2 tablespoons shredded coconut or cacao nibs

(optional)

Directions:

1.   In a food processor, pulse the macadamia nuts until they are a little smaller than rice size.

2.   In a bowl, combine the macadamia nuts, nut butter, erythritol, and butter and mix well. Add the shredded coconut or cacao nibs (if using) and stir well.

3.   Line a loaf pan using parchment paper then pour the mixture into the pan.

4. Refrigerate for 1 hour, remove, and cut into squares.

Keep in an sealed container, refrigerated or in the freezer.

Nutrition: Calories: 208 Total Fat: 21g Protein: 3g Total Carbs:

3g Fiber: 1g Net Carbs: 2g

Mozzarella Bagels

Preparation time: 30 minutes

Cooking time: 15 minutes

Servings: 6

Ingredients:

* 1 egg

* 1½ cups almond flour

* 1½ cup mozzarella, shredded

* 2 oz cream cheese, cut into pieces

* 1 tsp baking powder

* 1 tbsp oat fiber

Directions:

1. Put the mozzarella and cream cheese for 1 minute in a microwave. Stir and microwave for 30 seconds more.

2. In a food processor combine egg with microwaved cheese.

3. Add dry ingredients and process well. Scrape the dough out, wrap in plastic wrap, and place in the freezer for 20 minutes.

4.   Preheat oven to 400°F and line a baking sheet with parchment paper.

5.   Divide the dough into 6 portions.

6.   Make each piece into a sausage shape and seal the ends together forming a ring.

7.   Place on the parchment paper and bake for 12–15 minutes.

Nutrition: Calories: 245 Fat: 17g Carb: 5.6 g Protein: 7.2g

Cream Cheese Blueberry Muffins

Preparation Time: 10 minutes

Cooking Time: 12 minutes

Servings: 6

Ingredients:

- Nonstick cooking spray

- 1 cup almond flour

- 2 teaspoons ground cinnamon

- 3 to 4 tablespoons erythritol

- ¾ tablespoon baking powder

- 2 large eggs

- 2 tablespoons cream cheese

- 2 tablespoons heavy whipping cream

- 4 tablespoons butter, melted and cooled

- 2 teaspoons vanilla extract

- 2 tablespoons blueberries (fresh or frozen)

Directions:

1. Preheat the oven to 400°F. Spray a muffin tin using cooking spray or line it with muffin liners.

2. In a small bowl, put and mix the almond flour, cinnamon, erythritol, and baking powder.

3. In a medium bowl, place then mix the eggs, cream cheese, heavy cream, butter, and vanilla with a hand mixer.

4. Put the flour mixture into the egg mixture and beat with the hand mixer until thoroughly mixed.

5. Put the mixture into the prepared muffin cups.

6. Drop the berries on top of the batter in the muffin cups.

7. Bake for at least 12 minutes, or until golden brown on top, and serve.

Nutrition: Calories: 160 Total Fat: 15g Protein: 4g Total Carbs: 10g Fiber: 2g Net Carbs: 8g

Lunch recipes

Meatballs with Coconut Gravy

Preparation time: 20 minutes

Cooking time: 7 hours

Servings: 8

Ingredients:

- 3 tablespoons coconut

- 1 tablespoon curry paste

- 1 teaspoon salt

- 1 cup heavy cream

- 1 tablespoon flour

- 1 teaspoon cayenne pepper

- 10 oz. ground pork

- 1 egg

- 1 tablespoon semolina

- ½ cup onion, chopped

- 1 teaspoon kosher salt

- 3 tablespoons bread crumbs

- 1 teaspoon ground black pepper

Directions:

1. Combine the coconut, curry paste, and salt together.

2.   Add heavy cream and flour.

3.   Whisk the mixture and pour in the slow cooker. Cook on the LOW for 1 hour.

4.   Meanwhile, beat the egg in the big bowl and whisk.

5.   Add the cayenne pepper, ground pork, semolina, chopped onion, kosher salt, bread crumbs, and ground black pepper. Mix well and then make the small balls from the meat mixture and place them in the slow cooker.

6.   Coat the meatballs with the prepared coconut gravy and close the lid.

7.   Cook the dish for 7 hours on LOW. When the meatballs are cooked, serve them only with the coconut gravy. Enjoy!

Nutrition:

Calories: 312g,

Fat: 22g,

Carbs: 5g,

Protein: 34g,

Fresh Dal

Preparation time: 15 minutes

Cooking time: 5 hours

Servings: 11

Ingredients:

- 1 teaspoon cumin

- 1 oz. mustard seeds

- 10 oz. lentils

- 1 teaspoon fennel seeds

- 7 cups water

- 6 oz. tomato, canned

- 4 oz. onion

- ½ teaspoon fresh ginger, grated

- 1 oz. bay leaf

- 1 teaspoon turmeric

- 1 teaspoon salt

- 2 cups rice

Directions:

1.   Peel the onion. Chop the onion and tomatoes and place them in a slow cooker.

2.   Combine the cumin, mustard seeds, and fennel seeds in a shallow bowl.

3.   Add the bay leaf and mix. Sprinkle the vegetables in the slow cooker with the spice mixture.

4.   Add salt, turmeric, and grated fresh ginger. Add rice and mix.

5.   Add the lentils and water. Stir gently.

6.   Then close the slow cooker lid and cook Dal for 5 hours on LOW.

7.   When the dish is done, stir and transfer to serving plates. Enjoy!

Nutrition: Calories: 102g, Fat: 22g, Carbs: 5g,Protein: 34g,

Butternut Squash Soup

Preparation time: 10 minutes

Cooking time: 8 hours

Servings: 9

Ingredients:

- 2-pound butternut squash
- 4 teaspoon minced garlic
- ½ cup onion, chopped
- 1 teaspoon salt
- ¼ teaspoon ground nutmeg
- 1 teaspoon ground black pepper
- 8 cups chicken stock
- 1 tablespoon fresh parsley

Directions:

1. Peel the butternut squash and cut it into the chunks.

2. Toss the butternut squash in the slow cooker.

3. Add chopped onion, minced garlic, and chicken stock.

4. Close the slow cooker lid and cook the soup for 8 hours on LOW.

5.   Meanwhile, combine the ground black pepper, ground nutmeg, and salt together.

6.   Chop the fresh parsley.

7.   When the time is done, remove the soup from the slow cooker and blend it with a blender until you get a creamy soup.

8.   Sprinkle the soup with the spice mixture and add chopped parsley. Serve the soup warm. Enjoy!

Nutrition:

Calories 129,

Fat 2.7,

Fiber 2,

Carbs 20.85,

Protein 7

Eggplant Bacon Wraps

Preparation time: 17 minutes

Cooking time: 5 hours

Servings: 6

Ingredients:

- 10 oz. eggplant, sliced into rounds

- 5 oz. halloumi cheese

- 1 teaspoon minced garlic

- 3 oz. bacon, chopped

- ½ teaspoon ground black pepper

- 1 teaspoon salt

- 1 teaspoon paprika

- 1 tomato

Directions:

1.   Rub the eggplant slices with the ground black pepper, salt, and paprika.

2.   Slice halloumi cheese and tomato.

3.   Combine the chopped bacon and minced garlic together.

4.   Place the sliced eggplants in the slow cooker. Cook the eggplant on HIGH for 1 hour.

5.   Chill the eggplant. Place the sliced tomato and cheese on the eggplant slices.

6.   Add the chopped bacon mixture and roll up tightly.

7.   Secure the eggplants with the toothpicks and return the eggplant wraps back into the slow cooker. Cook the dish on HIGH for 4 hours more.

8.   When the dish is done, serve it immediately. Enjoy!

Nutrition:

Calories 131,

Fat 9.4,

Fiber 2,

Carbs 7.25,

Protein 6

Dinner Recipes

Chipotle Barbacoa

Preparation Time: 20 minutes

Cooking Time: 4 hours

Servings: 9

Ingredients:

- ½ c. beef/chicken broth

- 2 med. chilis in adobo (with the sauce, it's about 4 teaspoons)

- lb. chuck roast/beef brisket

- minced garlic cloves

- 2 tbsp. of each:

- Lime juice

- Apple cider vinegar

- 2 t. of each:

- Sea salt

- Cumin

- 1 tbsp. dried oregano

- 1 t. black pepper

- 2 whole bay leaves

- Optional: ½ t. ground cloves

Directions:

Mix the chilis in the sauce, and add the broth, garlic, ground cloves, pepper, cumin, salt, vinegar, and lime juice in a blender, mixing until smooth.

Chop the beef into two-inch chunks and toss it in the slow cooker. Empty the puree on top. Toss in the two bay leaves.

Cook four to six hrs. on the high setting or eight to ten using the low setting.

Dispose of the bay leaves when the meat is done.

Shred and stir into the juices to simmer for five to ten minutes.

Nutrition:

Calories: 242

Net Carbs: 2 g

Fat: 11 g

Protein: 32 g

Corned Beef Cabbage Rolls

Preparation Time: 25 minutes

Cooking Time: 6 hours

Servings: 5

Ingredients:

- ½ lb. corned beef
- large savoy cabbage leaves
- ¼ c. of each:
- White wine
- Coffee
- 1 large lemon
- 1 med. sliced onion
- 1 tbsp. of each:
- Rendered bacon fat
- Erythritol
- Yellow mustard

2 t. of each:

- Kosher salt
- Worcestershire sauce

¼ t. of each:

- Cloves

- Allspice

- 1 large bay leaf

1 t. of each:

- Mustard seeds

- Whole peppercorns

- ½ t. red pepper flakes

Directions:

1.   Add the liquids, spices, and corned beef into the cooker. Cook six hours on the low setting.

2.   Prepare a pot of boiling water.

3.   When the time is up, add the leaves along with the sliced onion to the water for two to three minutes.

4.   Transfer the leaves to a cold-water bath - blanching them for three to four minutes. Continue boiling the onion.

5.   Use a paper towel to dry the leaves. Add the onions and beef. Roll up the cabbage leaves.

6.   Drizzle with freshly squeezed lemon juice.

Nutrition:

Calories: 481.4

Net Carbs: 4.2 g

Protein: 34.87 g

Fat: 25.38 g

Main

German Style Soup

Preparation time: 10 minutes Cooking time: 8.5 hours

Servings: 6

Ingredients:

- 1-pound beef loin, chopped

- 2 cup water

- 1 cup sauerkraut

- 1 onion, diced

- 1 teaspoon cayenne pepper

- ½ cup Greek yogurt

Directions Put beef and onion in the slow cooker. Add yogurt, water, and cayenne pepper. Cook the mixture on low for 8 hours. Cook the soup on high for 30 minutes.

Nutrition : 137 calories, 16.1g protein, 4.3g carbohydrates, 5.8g fat, 1.1g fiber, 41mg cholesterol, 503mg sodium, 93mg potassium.

Herb Mixed Radish

Preparation Time: 10 minutes

Cooking Time: 3 hours

Servings: 4

Ingredients:

- cups of red radishes, halved
- ½ cup of vegetable broth
- 1 tablespoons of basil, diced
- 1 tablespoon of oregano, diced
- 1 tablespoon of chives, diced
- 1 tablespoon of green onion, diced
- A pinch of salt and black pepper

Directions:

Start by throwing all the ingredients into the Slow cooker.

Cover its lid and cook for 3 hours on Low setting.

Once done, remove its lid of the slow cooker carefully.

Mix well and garnish as desired.

Serve warm.

Nutrition:

Calories 266

Total Fat 26.9 g

Saturated Fat 15.8 g

Cholesterol 18 mg

Sodium 218 mg

Total Carbs 2.5 g

Sugar 0.4 g

Fiber 0.2 g

Protein 4.5 g

Tuscan Chicken

Preparation time: 15 minutes

Cooking time: 7 hours

Servings: 8

Ingredients:

- 1-pound chicken breast, skinless, boneless

- 1 tablespoon olive oil

- ½ cup full-fat cream

- 1 oz spinach, chopped

- oz Parmesan, grated

- 1 teaspoon chili flakes

- ½ teaspoon paprika

- 1 teaspoon minced garlic

- ½ teaspoon ground black pepper

Directions:

Chop the chicken breast roughly and sprinkle it with the chili flakes, paprika, minced garlic, and ground black pepper.

Stir the chicken and transfer to the slow cooker.

Add the full-fat cream and olive oil.

Add spinach and grated cheese.

Stir the chicken gently and close the lid.

Cook the chicken for 7 hours on Low.

Transfer cooked Tuscan chicken on the serving plates and serve!

Nutrition:

calories 136,

fat 7.2,

fiber 0.2,

carbs 1.4, protein 16

Corned Beef

Preparation time: 10 minutes

Cooking time: 8 hours

Servings: 6

Ingredients:

- 1-pound corned beef
- 1 teaspoon peppercorns
- 1 teaspoon chili flakes
- 1 teaspoon mustard seeds
- 1 bay leaf
- 1 teaspoon salt
- 1 oz bacon fat
- garlic cloves
- 1 cup water
- 1 tablespoon butter

Directions:

Mix the peppercorns, chili flakes, mustard seeds, and salt in the bowl.

Then rub the corned beef with the spice mixture well.

Peel the garlic and place it in the slow cooker.

Add the corned beef.

Add water, butter, and bay leaf.

Add the bacon fat and close the lid.

Cook the corned beef for 8 hours on Low.

When the corned beef is cooked, discard the bay leaf, then transfer the beef to a plate and cut into servings.

Enjoy!

Nutrition:

calories 178,

fat 13.5,

fiber 0.3,

carbs 1.3,

protein 12.2

Soups, Stews, and Chilis

Vegetable Beef Soup

Preparation time: 10 minutes

Cooking time: 4-6 hours

Servings: 6

Ingredients:

* pound lean ground beef

* 4 cups beef broth

* zucchini, diced

* stalks celery, chopped

* ½ cup diced tomatoes

* yellow onion, chopped

* cloves garlic, chopped

* 1 teaspoon freshly chopped thyme

* 1 teaspoon freshly chopped rosemary

* Salt & pepper, to taste

Directions:

1.   Add all the ingredients to a slow cooker and cook on high for 4 to 6 hours.

2.   Stir well before serving.

Nutrition: Calories: 185 Carbs: 5g Fiber: 1g Net Carbs: 4g Fat: 6g Protein: 7g

Lamb Taco Soup

Preparation time: 10 minutes

Cooking time: 4-6 hours minutes

Servings: 6

Ingredients:

- pound ground lamb
- 4 cups beef broth
- cup shredded cheddar cheese
- cup diced tomatoes
- 1 green bell pepper, chopped
- 1 yellow onion, chopped
- cloves garlic, chopped
- 1 teaspoon ground cumin
- 1 teaspoon ground coriander
- 1 teaspoon paprika
- ½ teaspoon cayenne pepper
- Salt & pepper, to taste

Directions:

1. Add all the ingredients to a slow cooker minus the shredded cheese and cook on high for 4 to 6 hours.

2.   Stir in the shredded cheese and serve.

Nutrition: Calories: 265 Carbs: 6g Fiber: 1g Net Carbs: 5g Fat: 13g Protein: 30g

Buffalo Sauce

Preparation Time: 10 minutes

Cooking Time: 30 minutes

Servings: 8

Ingredients:

- 8 ounces Cream Cheese (softened)

- ½ cup Buffalo Wing Sauce

- ½ cup Blue Cheese Dressing

- ½ cups Cheddar Cheese (Shredded)

- ¼ cups Chicken Breast (Cooked)

Directions:

1. Preheat oven to 3500F.

2. Blend together the buffalo sauce, white salad dressing, cream cheese, chicken, and shredded cheese.

3. Top with any other optional ingredients like blue cheese chunks.

4. Bake for 25-30 minutes

Nutrition: Calories: 325 Fat: 28g Carbs: 2.2g Protein: 16g

Hoisin Sauce

Preparation Time: 10 minutes

Cooking Time: 0 minutes

Servings: 8

Ingredients:

- 4 tablespoons low-sodium soy sauce

- 2 tablespoons natural peanut butter

- tablespoon Erythritol

- teaspoons balsamic vinegar

- teaspoons sesame oil

- teaspoon Sriracha

- garlic clove, peeled

- Ground black pepper, as required

Directions:

1. Put all together the ingredients in a food processor and pulse until smooth.

2. You can preserve this sauce in the refrigerator by placing it into an airtight container.

Nutrition: Calories: 39 Net Carbs: 1.2g Carbohydrate: 1.5g Fiber: 0.3g Protein: 1.8g Fat: 3.1g Sugar: 0.8g Sodi

Mexican Pot Roast

Preparation Time: 15 minutes

Cooking time: 8-10 hours

Servings: 4

Ingredients:

- 2 tablespoons olive oil

- 1 (4 pound) beef chuck roast, trimmed

- 1 teaspoon salt

- 1 teaspoon ground black pepper

- 1 large onion, chopped

- 1 (5 ounce) bottle hot sauce

- 1/4 cup taco seasoning

- 1 teaspoon garlic powder

Directions:

1. In a big skillet, heat the olive oil over medium-high heat. Use salt and pepper to season the beef chuck roast then cook it in hot oil for 2 to 3 minutes on each side. When it has browned entirely, move it to a slow cooker.

2.   Sprinkle garlic powder, cayenne pepper, chili powder, taco seasoning, hot sauce, chile pepper, and onion over the roast and cook it on low.

3.   Let it cook for 8 to 10 hours until the meat is fall-apart tender.

Nutrition: calories 231, fat 11, carbs 5, protein 10

Egg, Spinach, And Mushroom Slow Cooker Casserole

Preparation Time: 17 minutes

Cooking time: 8 hours

Servings: 5

Ingredients:

- 1 (24 ounce) carton cottage cheese

- 6 eggs

- 1/3 cup all-purpose flour

- 3 tablespoons chopped onion

- 2 tablespoons melted butter

- 1/2 teaspoon salt

- 1/4 teaspoon ground black pepper

- 2 cups shredded Cheddar cheese

- 1 (8 ounce) package sliced fresh mushrooms

- 1 (7 ounce) bag fresh spinach

Directions:

1.	In a bowl, stir together pepper, salt, butter, onion, flour, eggs, and cottage cheese. Stir in spinach, mushrooms, and Cheddar cheese.

2.	Into a slow cooker, put the mixture.

3.	Cook on Low with a cover, for 6 to 8 hours till eggs are firm.

Nutrition: calories 313, fat 16, carbs 9, protein 18

White Bean Soup with Shrimp

Preparation Time: 15 minutes

Cooking time: 6 hours 15 Minutes

Servings: 8

Ingredients:

- 2 strips thick-cut bacon, unflavored
- 1 large onion, diced
- 2 garlic cloves, minced
- 1-pound kale, washed and roughly chopped
- 1 cup dried barley
- 1 1/2 cups dried navy beans
- 6 cups low sodium chicken broth
- 4 cups water
- 8 oz. cooked shrimp

Direction:

1. Brown the bacon in a skillet over medium heat. When crisp, drain and transfer to slow cooker.

2. Drain off the drippings, leaving just enough to coat the skillet.

3. Sauté the onion and garlic until tender.

4.   Transfer to a slow cooker.

5.   Place kale, barley, and beans in the slow cooker.

6.   Pour in the broth and water, and stir.

7.   Cover and cook for 6-8 hours on LOW. Check occasionally to see if more water needs to be added.

8.   About 20 minutes before the end of cooking, add the cooked shrimps and stir to heat through. Serve and enjoy!

Nutrition: calories 149, fat 3, carbs 15, protein 16

Vegetables

Pecan Kale Mix

Preparation time: 15 minutes

Cooking time: 4 hours

Servings: 6

Ingredients

1 cup pecans, chopped

2 tablespoons butter, softened

1-pound kale, torn

¼ teaspoon salt

2 tablespoons cilantro, chopped

1 teaspoon turmeric

½ teaspoon onion powder

1/2 cup chicken stock

Directions:

1.   In the slow cooker, mix the kale with cilantro, pecans and the other Ingredients: and close the lid.

2.   Cook the mix on Low for 4 hours and serve.

Nutrition: calories 126, fat 4.8, fiber 4.6, carbs 6, protein 1.1

Mushroom Soup

Preparation time: 6 minutes

Cooking time: 7 hours

Servings: 4

Ingredients

- 1 cup cremini mushrooms, chopped
- 2 spring onions, chopped
- 1 garlic clove, diced
- 1 tablespoon oregano, chopped
- 1 teaspoon olive oil
- ¾ teaspoon ground black pepper
- 2 cups of water
- 1 cup of coconut milk

Directions:

1. In your slow cooker, mix the mushrooms with spring onions and the other Ingredients: and close the lid.

2. Cook the soup for 7 hours on Low.

3. When the soup is cooked, blend with an immersion blender and serve.

Nutrition: calories 214, fat 12...5, fiber 2.2, carbs 6.7, protein 2.3

Artichoke and Asparagus Mix

Preparation time: 15 minutes Cooking time: 2 hours

Servings: 4 Ingredients

- 2 artichokes, trimmed and halved
- 1-pound asparagus, trimmed and roughly chopped
- 2 spring onions, chopped
- 1 tablespoon almond butter
- ½ cup coconut cream
- ½ teaspoon salt
- 1 teaspoon chili pepper
- ¼ jalapeno pepper, minced
- ½ cup chicken stock

Directions: In the slow cooker, mix the artichokes with the asparagus, onion and the other Ingredients, close the lid and cook on Low for 2 hours.

Nutrition: calories 122, fat 5.9, fiber 4.5, carbs 5.2, protein 8.4

Lime Green Beans

Preparation time: 10 minutes

Cooking time: 2.5 hours

Servings: 5

Ingredients

- 1-pound green beans, trimmed and halved
- 2 spring onions, chopped
- 2 tablespoons lime juice
- ½ teaspoon lime zest, grated
- 2 tablespoons olive oil
- ¼ teaspoon ground black pepper
- ¾ teaspoon salt
- ¾ cup of water

Directions:

1.   In the slow cooker, mix the green beans with the spring onions and the other Ingredients: and close the lid.

2.   Cook for 2.5 hours on High.

Nutrition: calories 67, fat 5.6, fiber 2, carbs 4, protein 2.1

Cheese Asparagus

Preparation time: 10 minutes

Cooking time: 3 hours

Servings: 4

Ingredients

- 10 oz. asparagus, trimmed

- 4 oz. Cheddar cheese, sliced

- 1/3 cup butter, soft

- 1 teaspoon turmeric powder

- ½ teaspoon salt

- ¼ teaspoon white pepper

Directions:

1. In the slow cooker, mix the asparagus with butter and the other Ingredients, put the lid on and cook for 3 hours on High.

Nutrition: calories 214, fat 6.2, fiber 1.7, carbs 3.6, protein 4.2

Meat

Beef Roast

Preparation time: 10 minutes

Cooking time: 6 hours

Servings: 5

Ingredients

- 1-pound beef chuck roast

- 1 tablespoon ketchup

- 1 tablespoon mayonnaise

- 1 teaspoon chili powder

- 1 teaspoon olive oil

- 1 teaspoon lemon juice

- ½ cup of water

Directions

1   In the bowl, mix ketchup, mayonnaise, chili powder, olive oil, and lemon juice.

2   Then sprinkle the beef chuck roast with ketchup mixture.

3   Pour the water into the slow cooker.

4   Add beef chuck roast and close the lid.

5   Cook the meat on High for 6 hours.

Nutrition:

354 calories,

23.9g protein,

1.8g carbohydrates,

27.3g fat,

0.2g fiber,

94mg cholesterol,

119mg sodium,

230mg potassium.

Lunch Beef

Preparation time: 10 minutes

Cooking time: 8 hours

Servings: 2

Ingredients

- ½ white onion, sliced

- 1 teaspoon brown sugar

- 1 teaspoon chili powder

- 1 teaspoon hot sauce

- ½ cup okra, chopped

- 1 cup of water

- oz. beef loin, chopped

Directions

1   Mix the beef loin with hot sauce, chili powder, and brown sugar.

2   Transfer the meat to the slow cooker.

3   Add water, okra, and onion.

4   Cook the meal on Low for 8 hours.

Nutrition:

179 calories,

19.3g protein,

7.8g carbohydrates,

7.4g fat,

1.8g fiber,

53mg cholesterol,

520mg sodium,

146mg potassium.

Garlic Herb Pork

Preparation time: 10 minutes Cooking time: 8 hours

Servings: 10

Ingredients

- lbs. pork shoulder roast, boneless and cut into 4 pieces
- ½ tbsp. cumin
- ½ tbsp. fresh oregano
- 2/3 cup grapefruit juice
- garlic cloves
- Pepper and salt

Directions:

1   Add pork roast into the slow cooker. Season with pepper and salt. Add garlic, cumin, oregano, and grapefruit juice into the blender and blend until smooth. Pour blended mixture over pork and stir well. Cover slow cooker with lid and cook on low for 8 hours. Remove pork from the slow cooker and shred using a fork. Return shredded pork into the slow cooker and stir well. Serve warm and enjoy.

Nutrition: Calories 359 Fat 27.8 g Carbohydrates 2.1 g Sugar 1.1 g Protein 23.2 g

Garlic Thyme LambChops

Preparation time: 10 minutes Cooking time: 6 hours

Servings: 8

Ingredients

- lamb chops

- 1 tsp dried oregano

- 2 garlic cloves, minced

- ½ tsp dried thyme

- 1 medium onion, sliced

- Pepper and salt

Directions:

1   Add sliced onion into the slow cooker.

2   Combine together thyme, oregano, pepper, and salt.
Rub over lamb chops.

3   Place lamb chops in the slow cooker and top with garlic.

4   Pour ¼ cup water around the lamb chops. Cover slow
cooker with lid and cook on low for 6 hours. Serve and enjoy.

Nutrition: Calories 40 Fat 1.9 g Carbohydrates 2.3 g Sugar 0.6
g Protein 3.4 g Cholesterol 0 mg

Side Dish Recipes

Tarragon Sweet Potatoes

Preparation time: 15 minutesCooking time: 3 Hours

Servings: 4

Ingredients

- 1 pound sweet potatoes, peeled and cut into wedges

- 1 cup veggie stock

- ½ teaspoon chili powder

- ½ teaspoon cumin, ground

- Salt and black pepper to the taste

- 1 tablespoon olive oil

- 1 tablespoon tarragon, dried

- 2 tablespoons balsamic vinegar

Directions:

1.   In your Crock Pot, mix the sweet potatoes with the stock, chili powder and the other Ingredients, toss, put the lid on and cook on High for 3 hours.

2.   Divide the mix between plates and serve as a side dish.

Nutrition: calories 80, fat 4, fiber 4, carbs 8, protein 4

Classic Veggies Mix

Preparation time: 15 minutesCooking time: 3 Hours

Servings: 4 Ingredients

- 1 and ½ cups red onion, cut into medium chunks

- 1 cup cherry tomatoes, halved

- 2 and ½ cups zucchini, sliced

- 2 cups yellow bell pepper, chopped

- 1 cup mushrooms, sliced

- 2 tablespoons basil, chopped

- 1 tablespoon thyme, chopped

- ½ cup olive oil

- ½ cup balsamic vinegar

Directions:

1. In your Crock Pot, mix onion pieces with tomatoes, zucchini, bell pepper, mushrooms, basil, thyme, oil and vinegar, toss to coat everything, cover and cook on High for 3 hours.

2. Divide between plates and serve as a side dish.

Nutrition: calories 150, fat 2, fiber 2, carbs 6, protein 5

Green Beans and Mushrooms

Preparation time: 15 minutes

Cooking time: 3 Hours

Servings: 4

Ingredients

- 1 pound fresh green beans, trimmed

- 1 small yellow onion, chopped

- 6 ounces bacon, chopped

- 1 garlic clove, minced

- 1 cup chicken stock

- 8 ounces mushrooms, sliced

- Salt and black pepper to the taste

- A splash of balsamic vinegar

Directions:

1.   In your Crock Pot, mix beans with onion, bacon, garlic, stock, mushrooms, salt, pepper and vinegar, stir, cover and cook on Low for 3 hours.

2.   Divide between plates and serve as a side dish.

Nutrition: calories 162, fat 4, fiber 5, carbs 8, protein 4

Beans and Red Peppers

Preparation time: 15 minutes

Cooking time: 2 Hrs.

Servings: 2

Ingredients

- 2 cups green beans, halved
- 1 red bell pepper, cut into strips
- Salt and black pepper to the taste
- 1 tbsp. olive oil
- 1 and ½ tbsp. honey mustard

Directions:

1. Add green beans; honey mustard, red bell pepper, oil, salt, and black to Crock Pot.

2. Put on the cooker's lid on and set the cooking time to hours on High settings.

3. Serve warm.

Nutrition: Per Serving: Calories: 50, Total Fat: 0g, Fiber: 4g, Total Carbs: 8g, Protein: 2g

Appetizers & Snacks

Asparagus Bacon Bouquet

Preparation time: 15 minutes

Cooking time: 4 hours

Servings: 4

Ingredients

- asparagus spears, trimmed

- slices bacon

- 1 tsp black pepper

- Extra virgin olive oil

Directions:

1   Coat slow cooker with extra virgin olive oil.

2   Slice spears in half, and sprinkle with black pepper

3   Wrap three spear halves with one slice bacon, and set inside the slow cooker. Cook for 4 hours on medium.

Nutrition: Calories 345 Carbs 2 g Fat 27 g Protein 22 g Sodium 1311 mg Sugar 0 g

Creamy Asiago Spinach Dip

Preparation time: 15 minutes

Cooking time: 4 hours

Servings: 6

Ingredients

- cups spinach, wash, chopped

- ½ cup artichoke hearts

- ½ cup cream cheese

- ½ cup Asiago cheese, grated

- ½ cup almond milk

- 1 tsp black pepper

- Extra virgin olive oil

Directions:

1   Coat slow cooker with olive oil.

2   Place cream cheese and almond milk in a blender, and mix until smooth.

3   Finely chop spinach, add to blender along with salt and black pepper, and mix.

4   Place spinach mixture in a blender, add artichoke hearts and mix in with a spatula.

5	Sprinkle Asiago cheese on top, and cook on medium for 4 hours.

6	Serve dip with a selection of veggies like broccoli florets and carrot sticks.

Nutrition:

Calories 214

Carbs 4 g

Fat 19 g

Protein 8 g

Sodium 380 mg

Sugar 1 g

Madras Curry Chicken Bites

Preparation time: 15 minutes

Cooking time: 7 hours

Servings: 4

Ingredients

- 1 lb. chicken breasts, skinless, boneless

- cloves garlic, grated

- 1 tsp ginger, grated

- 2 cups low-sodium chicken stock

- 2 lemons, juiced

- 1 tsp coriander, crushed

- 1 tsp cumin

- ½ tsp fenugreek

- 1 tbsp. curry powder

- ½ tsp cinnamon

- 1½ tsp salt

- 1 tsp black pepper

- Extra virgin olive oil

Directions:

1   Cube chicken breast into ½" pieces, and sprinkle with ½ tsp salt and ½ tsp black pepper.

2   Heat 3 tbsp. extra virgin olive oil in a skillet, add chicken breasts, and brown.

3   Place chicken breasts in a slow cooker.

4   Add chicken stock, garlic, lemon juice, spices, and salt.

5   Cook on low for 7 hours.

Nutrition:

Calories 234

Carbs 3 g

Fat 8 g

Protein 38 g

Sodium 782 mg

Sugar 0 g

Spiced Jicama Wedges with Cilantro Chutney

Preparation time: 15 minutes

Cooking time: 4 hours

Servings: 8

Ingredients

- 1 lb. jicama, peeled

- 1 tsp paprika

- ½ tsp dried parsley

- 2 tsp salt

- 2 tsp black pepper

- Extra virgin olive oil

- Cilantro Chutney

- 1 tsp dill chopped

- ¼ cup cilantro

- ½ tsp salt

- 1 tsp paprika

- 1tsp black pepper

- 2 lemons, juiced

- ¼ cup extra virgin olive oil

Directions:

1   Slice jicama into 1" wedges, and submerge in a bowl of cold water for 20 minutes.

2   Place the paprika, oregano, salt, black pepper in a bowl, and toss with jicama.

3   Add 5 tbsp. extra virgin olive oil into a bowl and coat well.

4   Place jicama in the slow cooker, and cook on high for 4 hours.

5   Combine Ingredients for chutney in blender, mix, and refrigerate until jicama wedges are ready to serve.

Nutrition: Calories 94 Carbs 5.2 g Fat 8 g Protein 1 g Sodium 879 mg Sugar 1 g

Teriyaki ChickenWings

Preparation time: 15 minutesCooking time: 4 hours Servings: 4Ingredients:

- 2 lb. chicken wings
- 2 tsp ginger, grated
- cloves garlic, grated
- ¼ cup of soy sauce
- dates, pitted
- Extra virgin olive oil

Directions

1   Processed the dates in a food processor along with 2 tbsp. soy sauce, and mix until pasty.

2   Combine ginger, garlic, soy sauce, and dates in a bowl, add chicken wings, coat, and refrigerate overnight.

3   Coat slow cooker with a little sesame oil, add chicken wings and cook on high for 4 hours.

Nutrition: Calories 354 Carbs 5.5 g Fat 16 g Protein 45 g odium 730 mg Sugar 0 g

Portabella Pizza Bites

Preparation time: 15 minutes

Cooking time: 5 hours

Servings: 8

Ingredients

- Portabella Mushrooms

- ½ lb. ground pork

- 1 medium onion, diced

- cloves garlic, grated

- 2 cups crushed tomato

- ½ cup Mozzarella, shredded

- ¼ cup Parmesan

- ½ tsp oregano

- 1 tsp salt

- 1 tsp black pepper

- Garnish

- ½ cup parsley, chopped

Directions:

1   Coat 6 qt. slow cooker with extra virgin olive oil

2   Heat 3 tbsp. extra virgin olive oil in a skillet, add pork, brown.

3   Mix crushed tomato with salt, black pepper, oregano, parmesan, and garlic.

4   Spoon a little tomato-parmesan mixture into each mushroom, add a little ground pork, and sprinkle with Mozzarella.

5   Place each mushroom in a slow cooker. Cook pizza bites on medium for 5 hours.

6   Sprinkle a little parsley on top before serving.

Nutrition: Calories 106

Carbs 5.6 g Fat 3 g

Protein 13 g

Sodium 421 mg

Sugar 2 g

Desserts

Lemon Curd - Keto, Low Carb & Sugar-Free

Preparation Time: 3 minutes

Cooking Time: 13 minutes

Servings: 10

Ingredients:

•   1/2 cup fresh lemon juice

•   2 tablespoons Lemon zest

•   3/4 cup swerve confectioners (or erythritol)

•   1/4-pound grass-fed unsalted butter (at room temperature)

•   2 Whole eggs

•   3 Egg yolks

•   1/4 teaspoon salt

Directions:

1.   Add butter in a saucepan and stir in the swerve. Stir the eggs and the flour, lemon juice & zest for lemons. Switch the heat to medium-low, and simmer for 6-8 minutes until it thickens sufficiently to cover a spoon's back surface.

2.   The secret to smooth and fluffy coming out of this curd is to stir the whole time.

3.   Remove from heat and cover this with plastic wrap to ensure that it properly touches the curd. Chill out the refrigerator and relax.

Nutrition: Calories 376 Total Fat 11 g Total Carbs 2.9 g Sugar 5 g Fiber 13 g Protein 21 g

Easy Lemon Coconut Custard Pie with Coconut Milk

Preparation Time: 10 minutes

Cooking Time: 55 minutes

Servings: 8

Ingredients:

- Large eggs can use 3 for stiffer custard 3
- Coconut Milk canned 1 cup
- Low carb sugar 3/4 cup
- Coconut flour 1/4 cup
- Unsalted butter melted and cooled 2 tbsp.
- Vanilla extract 1 tsp.
- Baking powder 3/4 tsp.
- Lemon zest 1 tsp.
- Lemon Extract 1/2 tsp.
- Unsweetened Shredded Coconut 4 ounces

Directions:

1. Spray a cooking spray on a 9-inch pie dish and preheat oven to 350 degrees.

2.   Mix the ingredients, sweetener, coconut milk, coconut flour, sugar, baking powder, citrus zest, garlic, and lemon extract in a big dish. Stir until mixed.

3.   Fold in untreated hemp. Pour mixture into a serving platter.

4.   Bake for 40-45 minutes until it is crispy on the sides and a medium golden brown on top.

5.   Remove from oven and let it cool before trying to cut as well as serve.

6.   Keep the remaining in the fridge for up to three days.

Nutrition: Calories 23 Total Fat 12 g Total Carbs 3 g Sugar 5 g Fiber 12 g Protein 21 g

Keto Chocolate and Hazelnut Spread

Preparation Time: 12 minutes

Cooking Time: 10 minutes

Servings: 6

Ingredients:

- Hazelnuts 5 oz.

- Coconut oil 1/4 cup

- Unsalted butter 1 oz.

- Cocoa powder 2 tbsp.

- Vanilla extract 1 tsp.

- Erythritol 1 tsp.

Directions:

1. In a dry, hot frying pan, roast the hazelnuts until they develop a good golden color. Pay careful attention-the nuts can quickly burn. Let them cool a bit.

2. Place the nuts and roll them in a clean kitchen towel so that any of the shells fall off.

3. Put the nuts in a blender or food processor with the remaining ingredients. Mix in the desired consistency. The more you blend, the smoother the distribution.

Nutrition: Calories 195 Total Fat 14.3 g Total Carbs 4.5 g Sugar 0.5 g Fiber 0.3 g Protein 3.2 g

Keto Buttercream

Preparation Time: 12 minutes

Cooking Time: 15 minutes

Servings: 4

Ingredients:

- Unsalted butter 8 oz.

- Vanilla extract 2 tsp.

- Ground cinnamon 11/2 tsp.

- Erythritol 1 tsp.

Directions:

1. In a small saucepan, brown 1/4 of the butter before it becomes amber in color, but without burning.

2. Pour browned butter into a beaker and stir little by little with a hand mixer until it is moist in the remainder of the food.

3. Toward the end, add vanilla, cinnamon, and sweetener.

Nutrition: Calories 136 Total Fat 10.7 g Total Carbs 1.2 g Sugar 1.4 g Fiber 0.2 g Protein 0.9

Keto Caramel Sauce

Preparation Time: 3 minutes

Cooking Time: 1 hour

Servings: 4

Ingredients:

- Raw macadamia nuts or cashews 1/2 cup

- Coconut cream melted 1/2 cup

- Mito Sweet granulated erythritol and monk fruit sweetener, or liquid stevia to taste 1 tbsp

- Vanilla extract 3 tsp

- Grass-fed ghee melted 2 tbsp

- Pinch of salt

- Grain-Free Granola

- Creamy Coconut and Avocado Smoothie

- Dark Chocolate Trail Mix Bites

Directions:

1.   Preheat the oven to about 320 degrees.

2.   Put nuts on the baking tray, then toast them for 20 minutes in the oven, or until golden & crunchy.

3.   Allow the roasted nuts to cool slowly, then add them to a mixer and combine until smooth to most.

4.   Add rest of the ingredients, then blend until smooth. Be cautious not to over-blend because coconut cream will separate from it.

5.   If you would not use your keto caramel on the same day, place it in the refrigerator in a glass pan. Apply the material to a saucepan at medium heat and gently microwave to reheat to render it more pourable.

6.   Serve it with ice cream, or some gourmets treat

Nutrition: Calories 323 Total Fat 12 g Total Carbs 1 g Sugar 5 g Fiber 11 g Protein 25 g

Simple Low-Carb Chocolate Tart (Sugar-Free)

Preparation Time: 10 minutes

Cooking Time: 25 minutes

Servings: 8

Ingredients:

- Almond flour 1 1/4 cup

- Unsweetened shredded coconut 3/4 cup

- Medium egg 1

- Coconut cream 3/4 cup

- Coconut oil melted 1/4 cup

- Drops stevia or more

- Cacao powder unsweetened 2 tbsp and 1 tsp

- Vanilla essence 1 tsp

- Pinch of salt

- A small handful of chopped hazelnuts to garnish

Directions:

1.   Preheat oven about 180 centigrade.

2.   Mix almond flour, eggs, and shredded coconut in the food processor or stick blender until it shapes into a doughy ball.

3.   Press dough into a loaf tin that is covered with baking paper. On the sides, it should be about 2 fingers wide. To make it look good, press the corners with your fingertips if you wish.

4.   Bake the base tart for about 20 minutes, until its lightly browned. Take it out from the hot oven and allow cool.

5.   Now turn ganache into chocolate. Heat the coconut oil and then whisk in the cream of coconut, vanilla essence, cacao powder, pinch of salt, and powdered erythritol or stevia. If required, sample the sweetener and change it.

6.   Pour over the cool tart base & put in the refrigerator until completely set (about 1 1/2 hours).

7.   Until serving, on medium heat, dry roast a few sliced hazelnuts in the pan until golden.

Nutrition: Calories 32 Total Fat 7.2 g Total Carbs 1 g Sugar 3 g Fiber 0.7 g Protein 14 g

Easy Lemon Coconut Custard Pie with Coconut Milk

Preparation Time: 10 minutes

Cooking Time: 55 minutes

Servings: 8

Ingredients:

- Large eggs can use 3 for stiffer custard 3

- Coconut Milk canned 1 cup

- Low carb sugar 3/4 cup

- Coconut flour 1/4 cup

- Unsalted butter melted and cooled 2 tbsp.

- Vanilla extract 1 tsp.

- Baking powder 3/4 tsp.

- Lemon zest 1 tsp.

- Lemon Extract 1/2 tsp.

- Unsweetened Shredded Coconut 4 ounces

Directions:

1.   Spray a cooking spray on a 9-inch pie dish and preheat oven to 350 degrees.

2.	Mix the ingredients, sweetener, coconut milk, coconut flour, sugar, baking powder, citrus zest, garlic, and lemon extract in a big dish. Stir until mixed.

3.	Fold in untreated hemp. Pour mixture into a serving platter.

4.	Bake for 40-45 minutes until it is crispy on the sides and a medium golden brown on top.

5.	Remove from oven and let it cool before trying to cut as well as serve.

6.	Keep the remaining in the fridge for up to three days.

Nutrition: Calories 23 Total Fat 12 g Total Carbs 3 g Sugar 5 g Fiber 12 g Protein 21 g

CPSIA information can be obtained
at www.ICGtesting.com
Printed in the USA
BVHW060909250321
603396BV00008B/632

9 781801 948517